Unusual Pets

CHINCHILLAS

MARYSA STORM

BLACK RABBIT BOOKS

Bolt is published by Black Rabbit Books
P.O. Box 227, Mankato, Minnesota, 56002.
www.blackrabbitbooks.com

BOLT

Alissa Thielges, editor; Rhea Magaro, designer and photo researcher

Library of Congress Cataloging-in-Publication Data
Names: Storm, Marysa, author.
Title: Chinchillas / by Marysa Storm.
Description: Mankato, MN: Black Rabbit Books, [2026] | Series: Unusual pets | Includes bibliographical references and index. | Audience: Ages 8-12 | Audience: Grades 4-6
Identifiers: LCCN 2024043350 (print) | LCCN 2024043351 (ebook) | ISBN 9781644667781 (library binding) | ISBN 9781644667903 (ebook)
Subjects: LCSH: Chinchillas as pets—Juvenile literature. | Chinchillas—Juvenile literature.
Classification: LCC SF459.C48 S76 2026 (print) | LCC SF459.C48 (ebook) | DDC 636.935/93—dc23/eng/20250107
LC record available at https://lccn.loc.gov/2024043350
LC ebook record available at https://lccn.loc.gov/2024043351

Printed in the United States of America.

Image Credits

Alamy Stock Photo/Giel, O./juniors@wildlife, 4–5, 6–7; Dreamstime/Daizuoxin, 22, Diman Oshchepkov, 23, Dwori, 24, Katerina Grishekina, 21, Miraswonderland, 27, Verastuchelova, 22, Viorel Sima, 28–29; Shutterstock/Al More, cover, Anton Starikov, 25, Artem Kutsenko, 25, ATTILA Barsan, 16, Barbashova Sveta, 23, Creatopic, 1, 32, Ekaterina Krivtsova, 16, Eric Isselee, 18–19, Henrik Larsson, 12, Hlornet, 23, Irina Vasilevskaia, 26, ivector, 16, kesterhu, 22, Lewandowska_Malgorzata, 3, LittleDraw, 10, Litvalifa, 14–15, masa44, 23, New Africa, 25, Nils Jacobi, 13, Oleksandra Danilian, 25, Patrycja Skworc, 17, Prapat Aowsakorn, 22–23, Robyn Mackenzie, 25, Stas Ponomarencko, 15, Tahseenamjad, cover, valery.kruk, 9, Vitaly Soroka-Novitsky, 16–17, wallerichmercie, 25, yevgeniy11, 31
Every effort has been made to contact copyright holders for material reproduced in this book. Any omissions will be rectified in subsequent printings if notice is given to the publisher.

CONTENTS

CHAPTER 1

Meet the

A boy fills a shallow dish with dust. Then, he carefully picks up his chinchilla. He cradles the small, fluffy animal in his arms before setting it in the dish. Then, he steps back. His pet knows just what to do, and it's going to be dusty!

Bath Time!

The little **rodent** rolls and rolls. With each spin, it kicks up clouds of dust. The chinchilla's bushy tail sends dust everywhere. Eventually, the pet stops to shake it all off. That was a good bath!

Some people call chinchillas "chins" for short.

CHAPTER 2

There aren't many pets quite like a chinchilla. These rodents are super fluffy. In the wild, they live in South American mountains. There, they use their thick coats to stay warm.

Chins first came to the United States in 1923. At first, people **bred** them for their **pelts**. By the late 1900s, they were kept as pets.

Wild chinchillas are endangered.

WHERE CHINCHILLAS LIVE IN THE WILD

EUROPE
ASIA
AFRICA
AUSTRALIA
ANTARCTICA

Quiet Critters

Chins are mostly **nocturnal**. They prefer silence during the day. They're also quiet and often shy. This means they need gentle owners. If **stressed**, the rodents might lose fur! This is called a fur slip. Owners should be respectful of their chins. Some will like to cuddle, but others may not.

Chins should be kept away from other pets, especially cats. Cats might try to hunt them.

CHAPTER 3

Chinchilla

Chins have giant eyes. They have large, curved ears too. These give them excellent hearing. These little animals can't sweat. They don't do well in hot environments. Chins are slightly smaller than guinea pigs in size. Female chins are often bigger than males.

Average Size

LENGTH
8 to 14 INCHES
(20 to 36 cm)

0 1 2 3 4 5 6 7 8 9 10
pounds
pounds
WEIGHT
about
1 to 2
POUNDS
(0.5–1 kilogram)

LENGTH OF FUR

1.5 INCHES
(3.8 CM)

gray fur

bluish fur

Super Soft

Chinchillas are best known for their **plush** coats. Each chinchilla fur strand is about 1.5 inches (3.8 cm) long. Their fur comes in a few colors. They're often gray, white, or bluish. Beneath their thick fur is naturally oily skin.

white fur

PARTS OF A CHINCHILLA

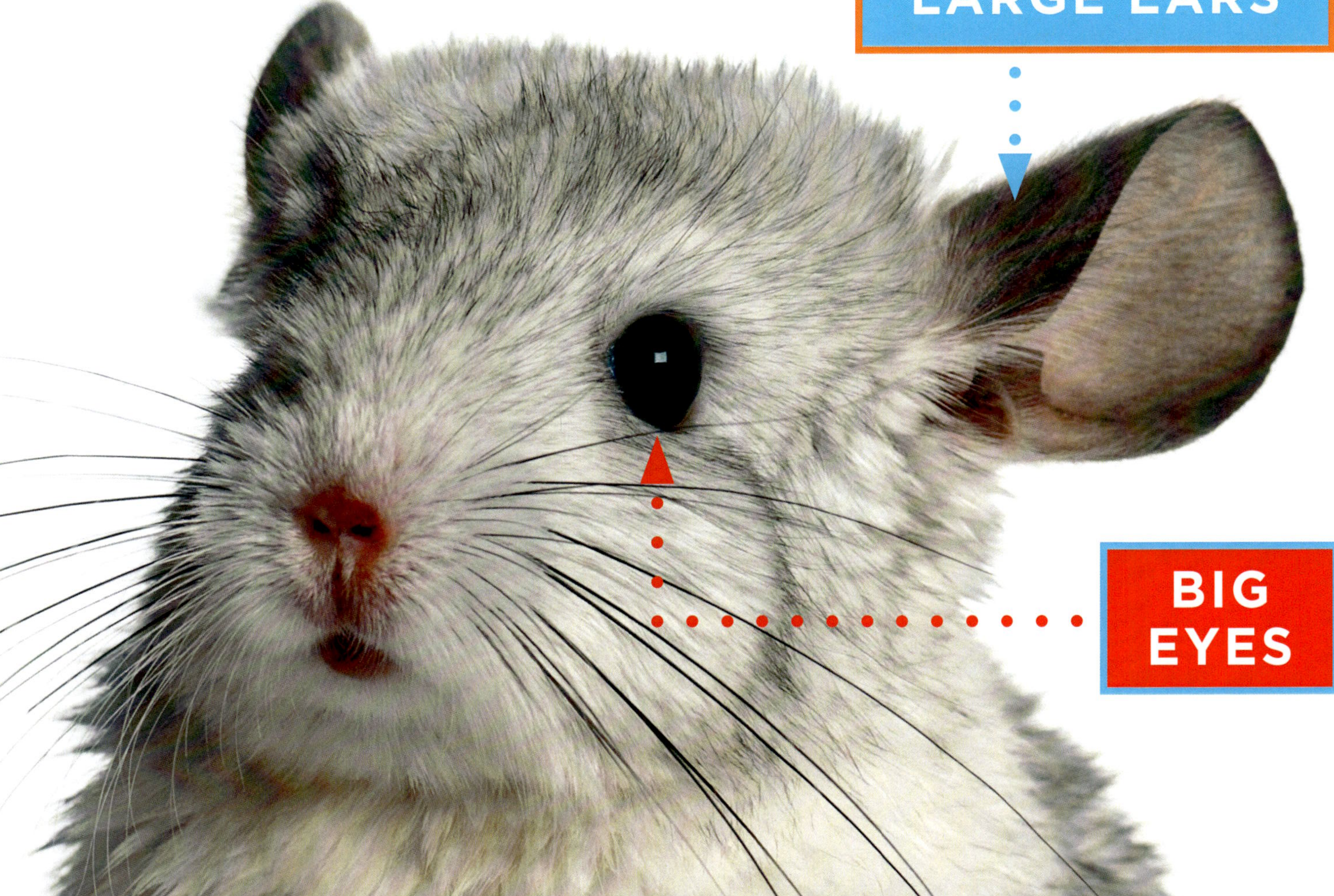

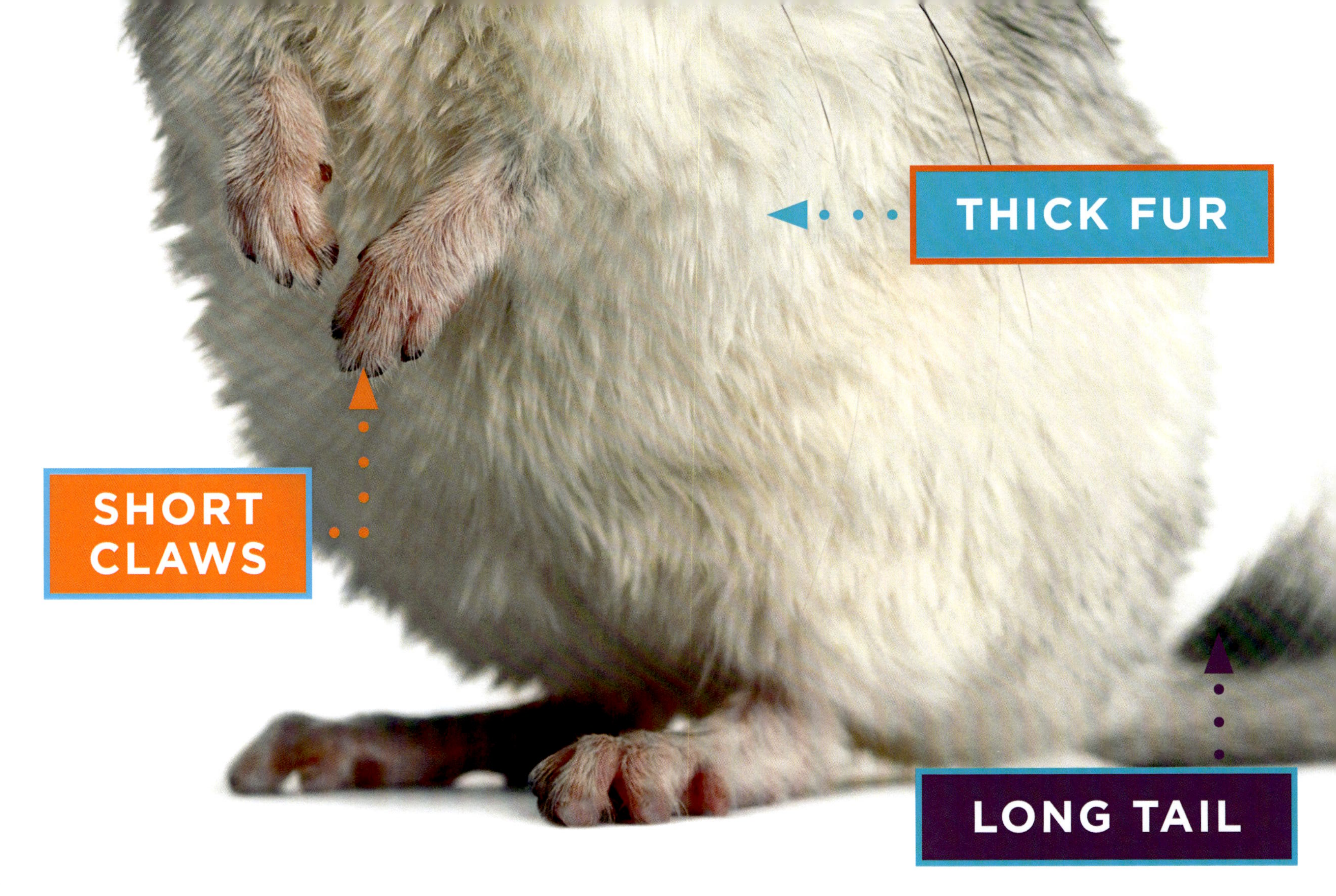
THICK FUR
SHORT CLAWS
LONG TAIL

CHAPTER 4

Caring for a CHINCHILLA

Chinchillas like to climb. Their cages should have multiple levels—and toys! A running wheel is great for a chinchilla. They should have a wood or **pumice** block too. Chewing on these blocks keeps their teeth sharp. It also wears them down. Rodent teeth never stop growing.

The cage should be wire with a solid bottom. A chin's foot could get caught in a wire bottom cage. It might get injured.

A CHINCHILLA ENCLOSURE

wheel

ramps

multiple levels

chewing block

food and water dishes
nest
toys

Food and Water

It's important for chinchillas to always have fresh water. When it comes to feeding, special chinchilla pellets are the best. They should have 1 to 2 tablespoons (15–30 milliliters) each day. Small amounts of hay, fresh vegetables, and some fruits are good too.

WHAT CAN CHINS EAT?

GOOD FOODS ✓

chinchilla pellets

leafy greens

hay

fruit (in small amounts)

BAD FOODS X

chocolate

caffeine

sugar

Special Care

Chinchillas need dust baths two to three times a week. The dust **absorbs** the oil on their skin. It helps clean their fur. Since chins can't sweat, owners must make sure these rodents don't overheat. Chinchillas make better pets for **experienced** owners. They need special care and a gentle touch. Would you be up for the challenge?

Owners should never bathe their chins in water. Their long fur takes too long to dry.

By the NUMBERS

65 to 80
degrees Fahrenheit
18 to 27 degrees Celsius

GOOD TEMPERATURE FOR CHINCHILLAS

10 to 20 YEARS

LIFE SPAN

about
6
feet
(1.8 meters)

HOW FAR THEY CAN JUMP

2

NUMBER OF CHINCHILLA BREEDS

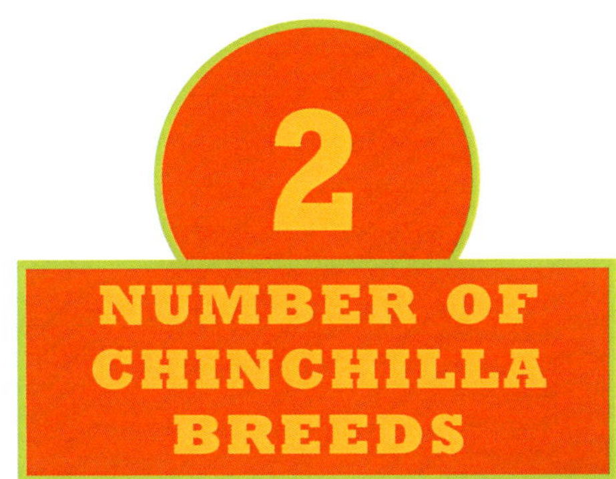

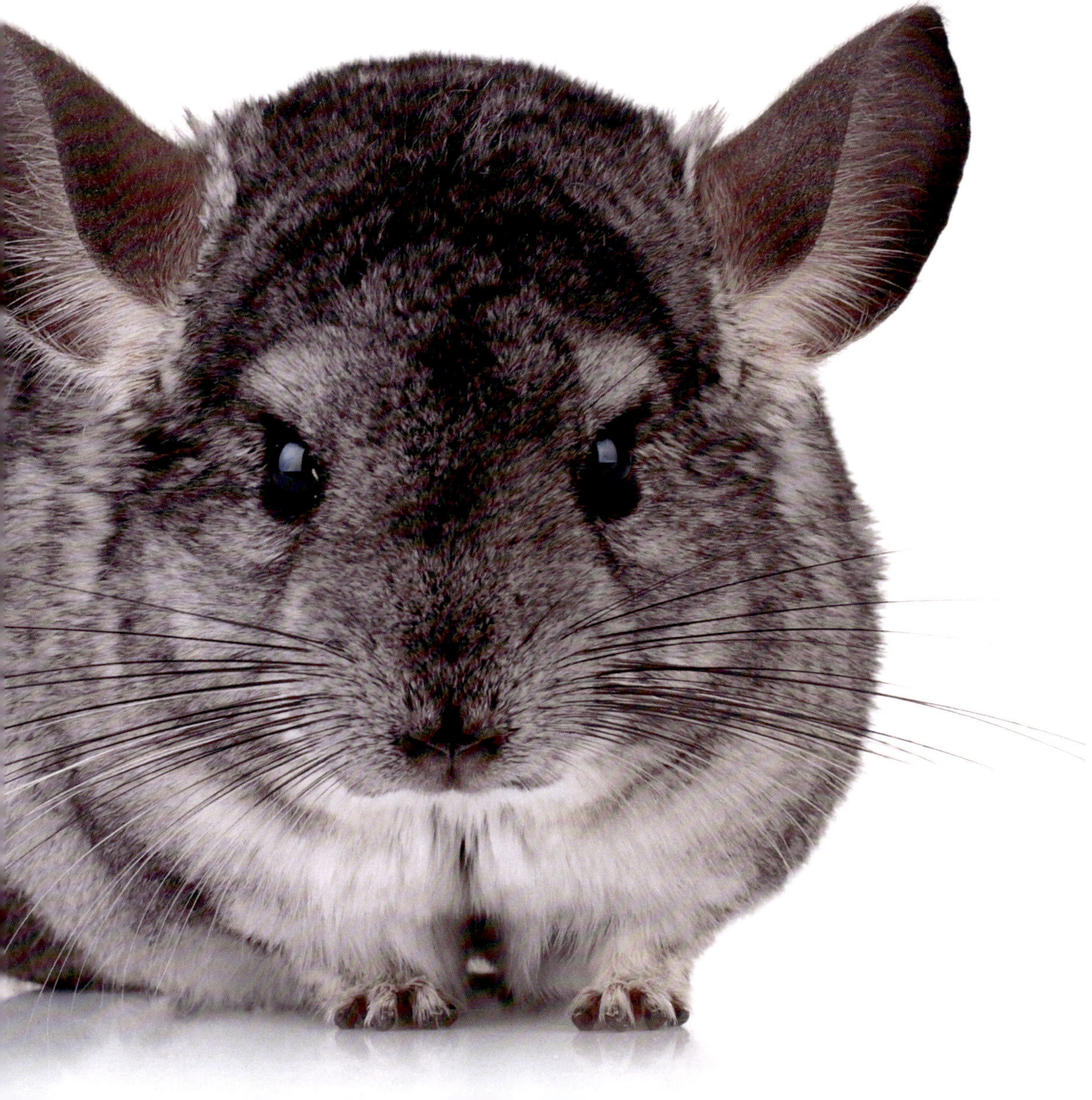

GLOSSARY

absorb (ab-SWARB)—to take in

bred (BREHD)—two specific animals that mated to create young with certain characteristics

experienced (ik-SPEER-ee-uhnst)—having skill or knowledge learned from doing something

nocturnal (NOK-turn-uhl)—active at night

pelt (PELT)—the skin of a dead animal with its hair or fur still on it

plush (PLUHSH)—thick and soft

pumice (PUHM-is)—a gray stone that is lightweight, full of small holes, and is used for smoothing and softening

rodent (RO-dent)—a small gnawing mammal, such as a mouse, squirrel, or beaver

stressed (STREST)—feeling very worried or anxious

BOOKS

Herschbach, Elisabeth. *Small Mammals.* Minneapolis: Abdo Publishing Company, 2024.

Mallory, Louis. *Do You Want a Pet Chinchilla?* Buffalo, NY: Enslow Publishing, 2025.

WEBSITES

5 Fun Facts about Chinchillas
www.petmd.com/exotic/fun-facts-about-chinchillas

Chinchilla
www.marylandzoo.org/animal/chinchilla/

Chinchillas
kids.britannica.com/students/article/chinchilla/273640

INDEX